SEA TURTLES

LIVING WILD

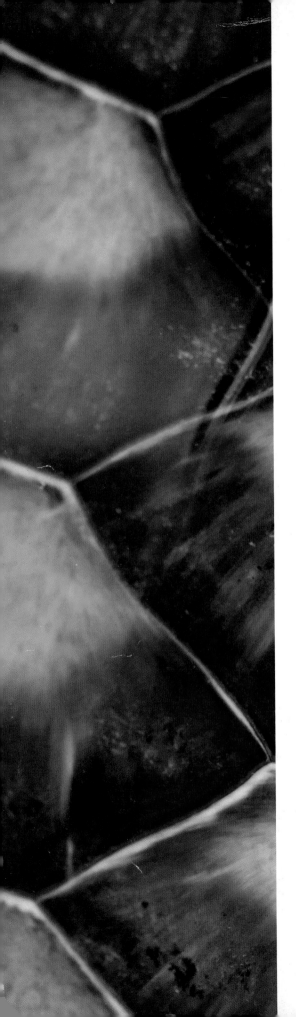

LIVING WILD

Published by Creative Paperbacks
P.O. Box 227, Mankato, Minnesota 56002
Creative Paperbacks is an imprint of The Creative Company
www.thecreativecompany.us

Design and production by Mary Herrmann
Art direction by Rita Marshall
Printed in the United States of America

Photographs by Alamy (AF archive, Reinhard Dirscherl, epa european pressphoto agency b.v., Frans Lanting Studio, Bill Gozansky, Travelpix, WaterFrame), Corbis (Jeffrey Rotman), Dreamstime (Mike Brake, Divehive, Hotshotsworldwide, Hronek, Idreamphotos, Ivkuzmin, Lighttouch, Olegd, Marty Wakat), iStockphoto (Mlenny, pigphoto), Shutterstock (AlexanderZam, Lynsey Allan, Greg Amptman, ARENA Creative, Kathryn Carlson, James A Dawson, Polly Dawson, fitkiwisparrow, Leonardo Gonzalez, Elliotte Rusty Harold, Isabelle Kuehn, Heather Nicaise, Pete Niesen, Stephanie Rousseau, StacieStauffSmith Photos, Bjorn Stefanson, Seree Tansrisawat, urciser, Leonard Zhukovsky), SuperStock (Minden Pictures, NHPA), Wikipedia (Rabon David/U.S. Fish and Wildlife Service, Claudio Giovenzana, National Park Service, NOAA, Purpleturtle57, Alexander Vasenin)

Library of Congress Cataloging-in-Publication Data
Gish, Melissa.
Sea turtles / Melissa Gish.
p. cm. — (Living wild)
Includes bibliographical references and index.
Summary: A scientific look at sea turtles, including their habitats, physical characteristics such as their shells, behaviors, relationships with humans, and protection of the swimming reptiles in the world today.
ISBN 978-1-60818-419-4 (hardcover)
ISBN 978-1-62832-005-3 (pbk)
1. Sea turtles—Juvenile literature. I. Title. II. Series: Living wild.

QL666.C536G5255 2014
597.92'8—dc23   2013031810

CCSS: RI.5.1, 2, 3, 8; RST.6-8.1, 2, 5, 6, 8; RH.6-8.3, 4, 5, 6, 7, 8

First Edition
9 8 7 6 5 4 3 2 1

SEA TURTLES

Melissa Gish

A full moon shines like a spotlight in the cloudless sky above Jekyll Island, Georgia.

The sandy beach is crisscrossed with the tracks
of newly hatched loggerhead sea turtles.

A full moon shines like a spotlight in the cloudless sky above Jekyll Island, Georgia. The sandy beach is crisscrossed with the tracks of newly hatched loggerhead sea turtles that have crawled from their nests and headed to the ocean. Many failed in this endeavor, falling prey to hungry seabirds and ghost crabs, but hundreds of hatchlings are now swimming with the current, their tiny bodies carried 80 miles (129 km) from shore toward the

Sargasso Sea. Chemical signals inside the turtles' brains act as a compass, directing the turtles to stay on course. The hatchlings swim for three days until they reach a dense carpet of floating seaweed. The turtles quickly seek cover beneath the thick canopy, poking their heads up for a quick breath every few minutes. Small shrimp and mollusks cling to the seaweed, providing food for the hungry hatchlings, whose tiny jaws snatch their first meals.

WHERE IN THE WORLD THEY LIVE

■ **Flatback Sea Turtle**
Australian coastlines

■ **Green Sea Turtle**
tropical Pacific, Indian, and Atlantic oceans

□ **Kemp's Ridley Sea Turtle**
Caribbean Sea to North Atlantic Ocean

■ **Loggerhead Sea Turtle**
Atlantic, Pacific, and Indian oceans; Mediterranean Sea

■ **Leatherback Sea Turtle**
oceans and seas from Norway to New Zealand

■ **Olive Ridley Sea Turtle**
tropical Pacific, Indian, and Atlantic oceans

■ **Hawksbill Sea Turtle**
tropical Pacific, Indian, and Atlantic oceans

The seven sea turtle species inhabit Earth oceans and seas between the Arctic and Southern oceans. The widest-ranging are the leatherbacks and loggerheads, while t flatbacks keep to the smallest area. Fame for their sometimes lengthy migrations and instinctual return to nesting sites, sea turtles are difficult to pin down. The color squares represent general areas in which they are found.

TURTLES OF THE SEA

Fossils of sea turtles have been found from as long ago as the Late Jurassic period, 208 to 144 million years ago.

Reptiles are one of the oldest groups of animals on Earth. As did their terrapin, tortoise, and freshwater turtle relatives, sea turtles inhabited Earth some 250 million years ago—long before many commonly known dinosaurs arrived. Because sea turtles have remained virtually unchanged for 150 million years, they and other reptiles like them have been termed "living fossils" by scientists. Sea turtles and their kin are members of the order Testudines, a name that comes from a Latin word meaning "shell." There are seven species of sea turtle. Six species (flatback, green, hawksbill, Kemp's ridley, loggerhead, and olive ridley) are members of the family Cheloniidae, or those with hard shells. The family Dermochelyidae contains only one member, the leatherback sea turtle, which has bony plates beneath the leathery skin on its back.

The top of a sea turtle's shell is called the carapace. Made up of about 50 bony plates called scutes, the carapace protects a sea turtle's muscled body. The plate on the underside of a sea turtle's shell is called the plastron, which is made up of nine softer bones. The two parts are held together by pieces of bone known as bridges. Carapace

Demand for its beautiful shell has made the hawksbill sea turtle the world's most endangered turtle species.

A sea turtle's shell is attached to the turtle's body—so the turtle can feel any touch on its shell as if it were skin.

colors vary by species. The ridley turtles both have olive-green-colored shells. The green sea turtle has a brown shell, as does the loggerhead, while the flatback's shell is olive-gray. The hawksbill, named for its tapered, birdlike head, has a strikingly dark amber shell with brown and black streaks. The leatherback's rubbery carapace is composed of a series of seven long ridges that are black with white specks.

Sea turtles' powerful, winglike, flippered limbs allow them to glide through the water. The largest sea turtle, the leatherback, is also the heaviest reptile. Weighing as much as 2,000 pounds (907 kg), the leatherback grows up to 8 feet (2.4 m) in length. Green and loggerhead turtles may be 450 pounds (204 kg) and 4 feet (1.2 m) long. Flatback and hawksbill turtles weigh nearly 200 pounds (90.7 kg) and attain lengths of between 35 and 39 inches (88.9–99 cm). The smallest species are the olive ridley and Kemp's ridley, which weigh no more than 100 pounds (45.4 kg) and have shells about 30 inches (76.2 cm) long.

Sea turtles do not have external ears. Instead, they have a membrane covering an inner ear. Like many birds, fish, and other reptiles, sea turtles have a see-through inner eyelid called a nictitating (*NIK-tih-tayt-ing*) membrane

The largest groups of olive ridleys gather along Costa Rican and Mexican coasts from July well into the wintertime.

Sea turtles nab jellyfish whenever possible, but many turtles die after eating plastic bags that resemble jellyfish.

that closes over each eye to protect the eyes when under water. Sea turtles' underwater vision is good, but above water, they have trouble seeing objects that are far away. Sea turtles have a highly sensitive sense of smell because of a special area on the roof of the mouth called the Jacobson's organ. This organ allows a sea turtle to detect the chemical signals given off by living things, which help it locate food.

Sea turtles cannot stick out their short, thick tongues to grasp food, and they do not have teeth. They use their hard beak to slice off mouthfuls of food or crush the shells of prey. The tongue is used to push food down the throat, which is lined with hundreds of cone-shaped papillae. The papillae hold the food in place, while throat muscles contract to squeeze out water and expel it before the food is swallowed. This keeps the sea turtle from drinking too much seawater.

Sea turtles' bodies get rid of the excess salt taken in from seawater through salt glands located at the base of the eyes. These glands operate similarly to tear ducts, making it look as though the turtles are crying. Many reptiles, including sea snakes and marine iguanas, have salt glands near their eyes, and seabirds such as albatrosses and gulls have salt glands around their nostrils for the same purpose.

Some kinds of seaweed contain more calcium than cheese, more protein than beef, and more vitamins than vegetables.

Green sea turtles eat **zooplankton**, small fish, and other tiny marine life while babies but become total herbivores with age.

Sea turtles raised on coastal farms are protected from the predators and normal dangers of the open sea.

Hawksbill turtle hatchlings typically hide under coral reef ledges and in caves, nibbling on sponges that grow there.

Unlike tortoises, which are land-dwelling, and turtles and terrapins, which spend only part of their lives in the water, sea turtles are fully aquatic. However, they must breathe oxygen. While actively swimming, sea turtles can hold their breath underwater for four to five minutes. When resting or sleeping, sea turtles slow down their body systems and stop using their lungs to breathe. This enables them to stay underwater for six hours or more. Then they rely on a method of respiration shared by frogs, sea snakes, and other aquatic creatures. This involves using the special tissue lining the mouth and throat like a sponge to extract oxygen from water as water passes over the tissues. The oxygen then makes its way throughout the turtle's bloodstream. Larger turtles can stay underwater longer than smaller turtles. Baby sea turtles sleep while floating on the water's surface with their front flippers pressed against their shells. Juveniles find seamounts on which to rest, and adults sleep wedged under ledges or coral reefs. Sea turtles also dive deep and remain inactive for as long as possible to avoid rough weather at sea.

Reptiles are ectothermic, meaning that their bodies depend on external sources of heat, and their body

To help it float, a sea turtle may fill its two pinkish, spongy lungs—located directly under the carapace—with air.

Sea turtles are among only four types of reptiles that continue to depend on the sea for survival.

temperatures change with the environment. To warm themselves, sea turtles swim near the water's surface to absorb the heat of the sun, and when they need to cool off, they dive deep—as far as 3,960 feet (1,207 m)—to reach cooler water. Extreme temperatures are dangerous for sea turtles. When water temperatures fall below 58 °F (14.4 °C) in northern waters, sea turtles move toward warmer southern waters. On the other hand, when turtles become too warm, they seek out cooler climates. The most favorable body temperature for a sea turtle is about 75 °F (24 °C). If a sea turtle's body temperature falls below 40 °F (4.4 °C) for a day, it will die of hypothermia (being too cold). Likewise, if its temperature rises above 100 °F (37.8 °C), it will die of hyperthermia (being too hot).

Problems with body temperature sometimes occur during nesting, which is done on land at night. If a turtle does not finish nesting by dawn, it can become stranded on a beach and quickly perish in the sun. Every year, sea turtle rescue centers and marine animal hospitals around the world take in stranded turtles suffering from temperature-related health issues.

Loggerhead turtles frequently feed on horseshoe crabs, which they dig up from burrows in the seabed.

On average, loggerhead turtles travel 9,000 miles (14,484 km) to nest—one of the longest migrations of any animal.

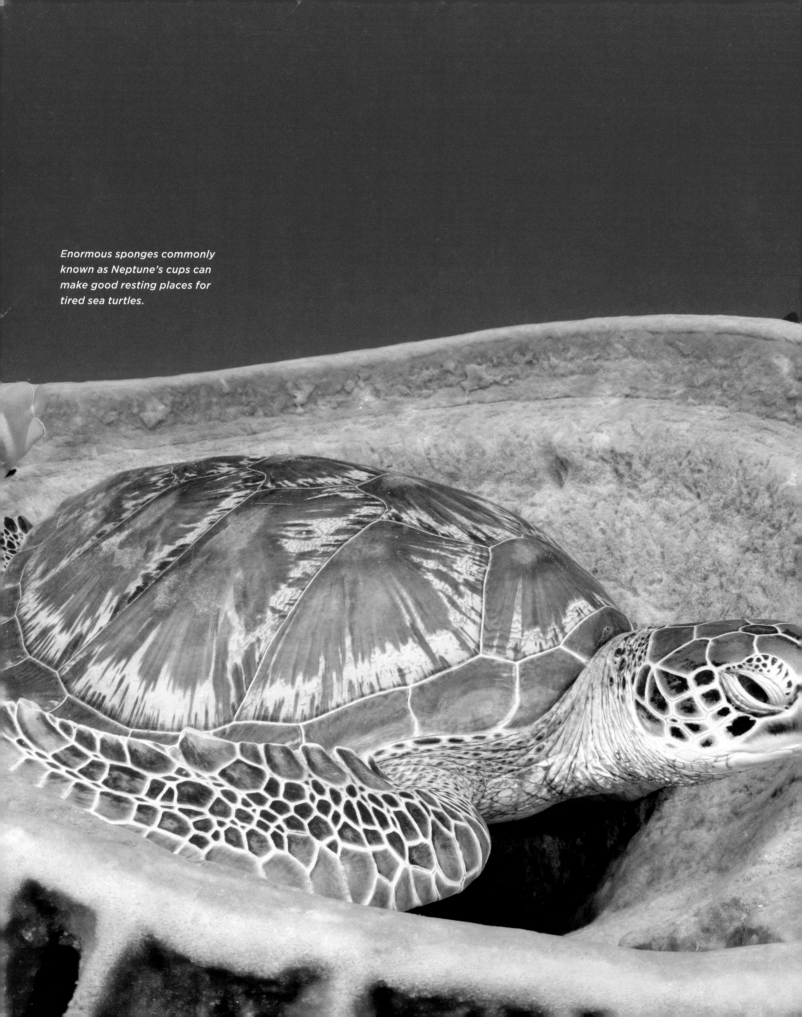

Enormous sponges commonly known as Neptune's cups can make good resting places for tired sea turtles.

OCEAN WANDERERS

Like many reptiles, sea turtles have long life spans—as long as 100 years, depending on the species. From the time a sea turtle hatches until the age of 10, it will have grown as much as 70 times larger. Olive and Kemp's ridley sea turtles are old enough to mate at 7 to 15 years old, and loggerheads mate when they reach 20 to 30 years. Green sea turtles take 10 to 59 years to mature! Maturity is related to carapace size, and the rate at which a sea turtle's carapace grows is determined by factors such as food availability and environmental stress.

Sea turtles have habitat-specific diets. As deep-water travelers in every ocean on the planet except the Arctic and Southern, leatherback turtles feed almost exclusively on jellyfish that drift with the currents. Kemp's ridleys range from the Caribbean Sea to the North Atlantic, feeding on clams, crabs, and sea snails in coastal waters less than 150 feet (45.7 m) deep. Olive ridleys and loggerheads have a similar diet, but they are found all across the tropical waters of the Pacific, Indian, and Atlantic oceans. Hawksbills are members of tropical coral reef societies and feed almost exclusively on sponges

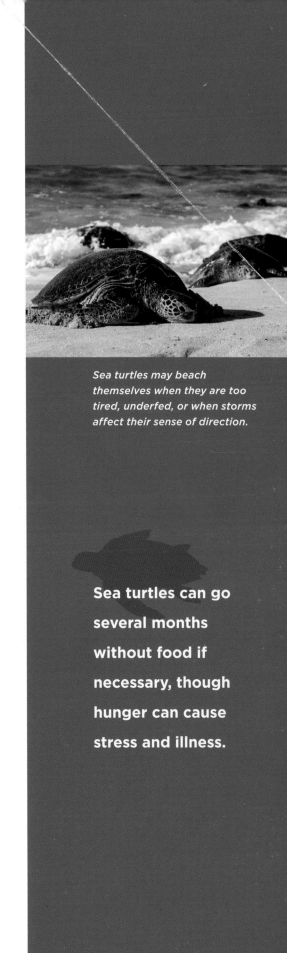

Sea turtles may beach themselves when they are too tired, underfed, or when storms affect their sense of direction.

Sea turtles can go several months without food if necessary, though hunger can cause stress and illness.

Sea turtles keep their coral reef habitats balanced by eating sponges before the invertebrates can overcrowd the surroundings.

anchored to the reef or the seafloor, while flatbacks are found only in the coastal waters of Australia, feeding on **invertebrates** such as sea cucumbers and squids. Green sea turtles, the only herbivores among sea turtles, are named for the green layer of fat beneath their carapace. Green sea turtles share habitat with olive ridleys.

Like most reptiles, sea turtles reproduce by laying eggs, and these eggs are laid and hatch on land. When instinct drives sea turtles to mate, they typically return to the beaches where they hatched, gathering together offshore. Research has revealed that sea turtles are able to navigate, or orient

themselves and find their way, by sensing variations in the strength of Earth's **magnetic field**, which is strongest at the poles and weakest at the equator (the imaginary line that separates the Northern and Southern Hemispheres).

Mating is done either underwater or while floating on the water's surface. Males and females of the same species are virtually identical, except that mature males have a longer, thicker tail, which is used in reproduction. Males court females by nudging the head or nipping the neck and rear flippers. When a female is responsive, a male positions himself on top of the female's shell, and his long

Once a female sea turtle has dug her nest and begun laying eggs, she enters a trancelike state and should not be disturbed.

tail wraps underneath her. After he fertilizes the female's eggs, the male goes back to the open ocean. A female may mate with several males, storing the **genetically** diverse reproductive material in her body for up to several months while making her way to her nesting ground or waiting for weather conditions to be favorable for nesting. Female sea turtles mate only every two to four years.

Most sea turtles nest during the warmest summer months of the year. (In the Northern Hemisphere, summer is June through August, and in the Southern Hemisphere, it is December through February.) The nesting period for a female sea turtle begins with site selection. The female waits until nighttime to leave the water and cross a sandy beach to a spot that will be high enough to remain dry. She uses her hind flippers to dig a hole about 17 inches (43.2 cm) deep. Depending on the species, the turtle will lay 50 to 200 eggs that look like Ping-Pong balls. The eggs are flexible and leathery when laid, but the shells harden over a period of several weeks. The turtle then covers the hole and pats down the sand with her flippers before returning to the sea. She may never see her hatchlings again, and if she does, she will not recognize them as her offspring.

Throughout the nesting period, a sea turtle may return to land every two weeks or so and as often as nine times, digging a new nest to lay another batch of eggs, called a clutch. A single sea turtle may lay up to 1,400 eggs in a season. Most sea turtle species, including the hawksbill, practice dispersed nesting, which means they arrive on nesting beaches alone or in small groups. The ridleys, on the other hand, are known for mass-nesting events called "arribadas" (Spanish for "arrivals"). Because mother turtles return to the sea after laying eggs, their nests are left unguarded for the 60 to 80 days that it takes for the eggs to **incubate**. While it is illegal in most countries to disturb a

Because sea turtle eggs are soft, they are not damaged as they fall into a deep, sandy hole.

In 2008, a leatherback turtle set the record for longest sea animal migration: 12,774 miles (20,558 km) in 647 days.

Emergence from the nest and the journey to sea is the most perilous time in a sea turtle's entire life.

sea turtle nest, **poaching** does occur in some isolated places. However, many beaches around the world are fenced and even patrolled to protect the nests.

About two-thirds of the way through the incubation process, the level of heat in the nest will determine the gender of the offspring. While exact temperatures vary by species, in general, temperatures above 86 °F (30 °C) produce females and temperatures below 82 °F (27.8 °C) produce males. In large clutches, the eggs closest to the center of the nest are warmer and therefore produce females, while the eggs around the outer edges typically produce males.

When it begins developing inside the egg, a baby turtle is folded in half, nose to tail. As it grows, it straightens out, and an egg tooth develops on the tip of its snout. This sharp projection enables the hatchling to slice through the egg's leathery interior membrane and break through the shell. The egg tooth wears away soon afterward. Hatchlings are about two inches (5.1 cm) long. They typically wait under the sand for all of their siblings to hatch, and then as a group they begin digging their way out of the nest. Occasionally, the turtles emerge in

daylight, but typically they wait until dark—when they feel the air temperature grow cooler above them—before emerging from beneath the last layer of sand. When they burst forth, the hatchlings immediately orient themselves toward the brightest light they can see—the moon reflecting on the ocean—and make a mad dash for the water. Falling prey to crabs, seabirds, and other predators, more than 30 percent of the hatchlings will die before reaching the ocean, and, once there, only 1 in 4,000 will survive to reproductive age.

Sea turtles cannot see red light, so in order to avoid disturbing these animals, observers use red flashlights.

Paul DiPasquale's Neptune holds pet loggerhead in one hand and a trident in the other on the Virginia Beach Boardwalk.

THE LIVING COMPASS

Since the earliest human **cultures** first inhabited islands and coastlines, sea turtles have had strong cultural links to these people. Among the Olmecs of **Mesoamerica**, the sea turtle was respected as both a food source and for being closely tied to the Olmecs' understanding of magnetism and navigation. To Olmecs, a swimming turtle represented the very structure of the world, with its shell as the earth and its body in the waters beneath. The Olmecs, whose cities bordered the Gulf of Mexico from about 1400 to 400 B.C., seemed to understand that sea turtles had special powers of navigation. Around 1000 B.C., at Izapa, a site in southern Mexico, the Olmecs sculpted a sea turtle head out of a rock containing large amounts of magnetic iron ore. The lines carved on its face, all pointing toward the turtle's snout, appeared to represent magnetic field lines, or the invisible "lines" that guide the movement of a magnet. Researchers who studied the sculpture in 1975 interpreted it this way, arguing that the Olmecs knew that sea turtles used magnetic force to find their way back to their home beaches for nesting. Three other sea turtle sculptures are located at Izapa: one of them,

Mexico City's National Museum of Anthropology exhibits thousands of objects from pre-Hispanic history.

Turtle Tomb near Sipadan, Spain, contains skeletons of sea turtles that drowned in a maze of underwater caves.

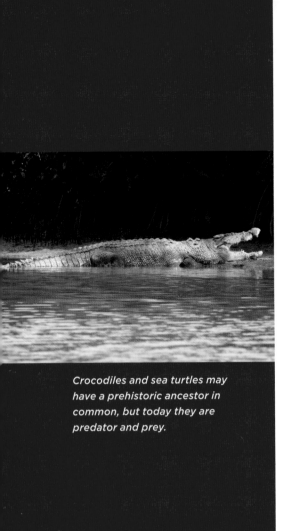

Crocodiles and sea turtles may have a prehistoric ancestor in common, but today they are predator and prey.

Australia's saltwater crocodiles may travel out to sea to eat sea turtles, crushing through shells with their forceful bite.

when filled with water that floats a needle, could be used as a crude compass. Another was used as a ceremonial altar.

Archaeologists working in the Middle East found some of the earliest evidence of human reliance on sea turtles at a number of ancient sites. Sea turtle bones and other artifacts from more than 7,000 years ago revealed that when green sea turtles left the waters of the Persian Gulf and the Gulf of Oman to come ashore for nesting, people captured them for their meat and shells and also dug up the turtle eggs for food. Shell **middens** and burned turtle bones and shells found at sites near Ras al Hadd, a coastal village in Oman, indicate that more than 2,000 years ago, not only were turtles used in religious ceremonies, but their oil was also used for fuel. To this day, the beaches at Ras al Hadd and nearby Ras al-Jinz are known as being breeding grounds for green sea turtles and are protected as such.

An ancient Chinese story from the 4th century B.C. tells how, once, all the water in the world flowed into a bottomless pool. In the pool floated the five highest mountains, where the gods lived. Because the mountains were not rooted in the earth, they crashed around on the waves and caused much chaos. Yuqiang, the god of the wind

and the northern sea, was asked to remedy the situation. He called forth from the ocean 15 great sea turtles and arranged them into groups of 3. Each turtle would take turns holding each of the mountains on its head for a period of 60,000 years. After all the turtles had taken a turn, the mountains remained rooted on the bottom of the sea.

Chinese folklore depicts the cheerful monk, Budai, sharing his happiness with the creatures of the world—including sea turtles.

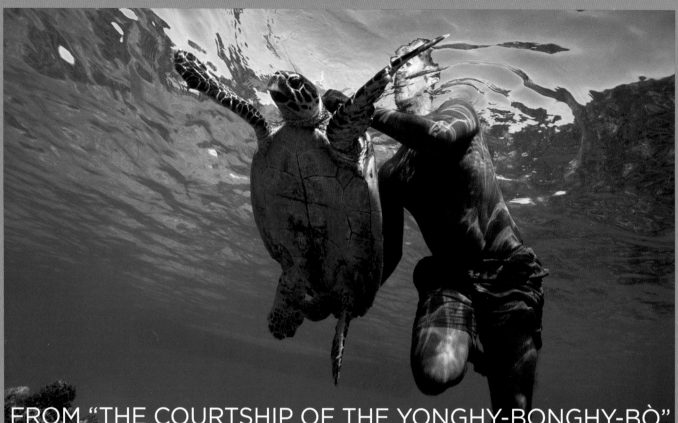

FROM "THE COURTSHIP OF THE YONGHY-BONGHY-BÒ"

VIII.
Down the slippery slopes of Myrtle,
Where the early pumpkins grow,
To the calm and silent sea
Fled the Yonghy-Bonghy-Bò.
There beyond the Bay of Gurtle,
Lay a large and lively Turtle;—
"You're the Cove," he said, "for me;
"On your back beyond the sea,
"Turtle, you shall carry me!"
Said the Yonghy-Bonghy-Bò.
Said the Yonghy-Bonghy-Bò.

IX.
Through the silent-roaring ocean
Did the Turtle swiftly go;
Holding fast upon his shell
Rode the Yonghy-Bonghy-Bò,
With a sad primæval motion
Towards the sunset isles of Boshen
Still the Turtle bore him well,
Holding fast upon his shell.
"Lady Jingly Jones, farewell!"
Sang the Yonghy-Bonghy-Bò,
Sang the Yonghy-Bonghy-Bò.

X.
From the Coast of Coromandel
Did that Lady never go;
On that heap of stones she mourns
For the Yonghy-Bonghy-Bò.
On that Coast of Coromandel,
In his jug without a handle,
Still she weeps, and daily moans;
On that little heap of stones
To her Dorking Hens she moans
For the Yonghy-Bonghy-Bò,
For the Yonghy-Bonghy-Bò.

by Edward Lear (1812–88)

According to Hindu tradition, the sea turtle carries four elephants on its shell, and the elephants hold up the world. The elephants walk in a circle, causing the planet to spin. When they stumble, they create earthquakes. The sea turtle swims in a circle, making waves in the oceans. When the sea turtle splashes its flippers, it creates tidal waves and **monsoons**.

Images of sea turtles were stamped onto ancient Greek coins from 2,700 years ago, and early Greek sailors told stories that became part of enduring legends about mysterious sea turtles that rescued sailors who fell overboard or carried shipwrecked survivors to islands. Sea turtles have also been depicted on modern currency and coins, including a coin minted in the Republic of Maldives, an island nation in the Indian Ocean, in 1984. Around the world, sea turtles have appeared on postage stamps in dozens of countries, including Malawi, the Caribbean island of Bequia, and Mayotte, a French-controlled island off the eastern coast of Africa.

Since 1991, an animated sea turtle named Fillmore, featured in the comic strip *Sherman's Lagoon*, has appeared daily in more than 150 newspapers worldwide. Fillmore

Australia considers the flatback sea turtle, found nowhere else on Earth, one of its national treasures.

Sea turtles may rub against rocks to scratch off parasites—much like bears rubbing themselves on trees.

Sea turtles regularly visit coral reefs to allow small surgeonfish and wrasse to clean parasites off their bodies.

spends his time reading novels, watching operas, and caring for his adopted son Clayton. Other turtle characters are featured in a host of iPad® and iPhone® games, including "Turtle Isle," in which players help sea turtles safely come ashore to lay eggs, and "Turtle Frenzy," in which players help hatchlings dash to the ocean.

The 2003 Pixar movie *Finding Nemo* features a group of green sea turtles riding the East Australian Current (EAC). Many species of fish and marine animals gather in this powerful ocean current, which flows at up to eight miles (13 km) per hour, and are carried down the eastern coast of Australia. In *Finding Nemo*, the green sea turtle Crush and his young son Squirt invite Nemo's father to join them on the current, riding the rushing water like surfers on a wave. Crush and Squirt are endearing characters that appear in a variety of media, from the online game "Cruisin' with Crush" to Crush's own show "Turtle Talk with Crush," which plays at all the major Disney resorts. Crush is also featured in a number of Disney park attractions, including "Finding Nemo: The Musical" at Disney's Animal Kingdom and "The Seas with Nemo and Friends" at Disney World's Epcot Center.

Finding Nemo characters take advantage of the EAC, which, in real life, is strongest during the Southern Hemisphere's summer.

Another animated sea turtle is featured in *A Turtle's Tale: Sammy's Adventures*, a 3D movie made in Belgium and released in North America in 2010 by Studio Canal. The movie follows Sammy the green sea turtle through 50 years of his life as he finds his way across the seas and witnesses many gradual changes to the planet's oceans—the results of global warming. A real-life loggerhead turtle is the star of SeaWorld Pictures' 3D movie *Turtle: The Incredible Journey* (2009). The film documents the turtle's story from her hatching on a Florida beach and as she grows up. The movie shows the turtle facing many dangers around the world, such as fishermen and sharks, and encountering many wonders of the sea, including sperm whales working together to capture fish.

Remoras are harmless fish that use their sucker-like mouths to hitch a ride on other sea creatures as they travel.

AN UNCERTAIN FUTURE

Because sea turtles are so widely dispersed, difficult to track, and impossible to observe for extended periods, **herpetologists'** knowledge of them is far from complete. Even known facts are still somewhat mysterious. In 1976, biologists found a small population of sea turtles near Baja California, Mexico, **hibernating**. This was contrary to typical sea turtle behavior. Four years later, a second hibernating group of sea turtles was found off the coast of Cape Canaveral, Florida. Why only these two groups of turtles hibernate is unclear. Further, the turtles do not hibernate every year, and researchers have been unsuccessful in making accurate predictions as to whether they will choose to hibernate. Current studies suggest that when the water temperature remains between 47 and 59 °F (8.3 to 15 °C) for an extended period of time, the turtles either hibernate or follow other turtles to warmer climates.

What researchers do know about sea turtles may not be enough to save the animals from dying out. Sea turtles face enormous threats from pollution, **commercial** fishing, poaching, boats, artificial lighting that occurs with beach development, and the effects of climate change. Research

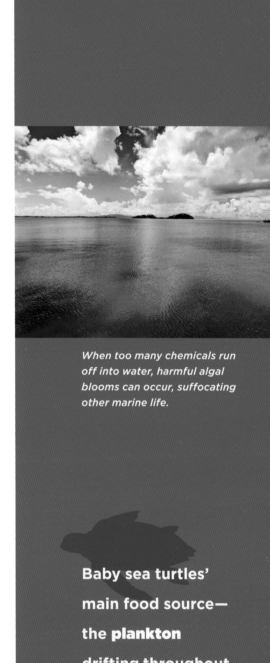

When too many chemicals run off into water, harmful algal blooms can occur, suffocating other marine life.

Baby sea turtles' main food source— the plankton drifting throughout the oceans—makes up half the life on Earth.

The most common threats to adult sea turtles are posed by commercial fishing nets and beach development near nesting sites.

into conservation methods is being conducted around the world. Most sea turtle studies are conducted at beach sites, where nesting females and hatchlings are more easily accessible to researchers. New technologies such as satellite tracking are enabling offshore research to be conducted as well. Rescued and rehabilitated sea turtles can be fitted with a temporary **Global Positioning System** (GPS) device on their carapace. Over a period of months or years, the device sends an electronic signal that can be picked up by a weather satellite and used to track movement—information that may be useful in efforts to conserve sea turtles.

Many zoos and aquariums, including the Georgia Aquarium in Atlanta and the Aquarium of the Pacific in Long Beach, California, are involved in sea turtle tracking and share their information with SeaTurtle.org, a website devoted to sea turtle research and education. A number of sea turtles are listed in the site's tracking directory, and visitors to the site can participate in the tracking of sea turtles as well as many other animals currently being researched.

Many organizations have been studying the effects of the Deepwater Horizon oil spill, one of the worst marine disasters in history. For three months in 2010, millions of

barrels of crude oil poured from a damaged well in the Gulf of Mexico. Marine life in the area was devastated then and continues to suffer the effects today. The Archie Carr Center for Sea Turtle Research at the University of Florida has been studying the remains of hundreds of sea turtles killed by the oil spill and gathering data on organ and tissue damage to determine how sea turtle populations continue to be affected by the oil spill.

In addition to oil spills, pollution in the form of chemicals and waste change the balance of **nutrients** in the ocean, leading to an increase in parasites and viruses. One virus that afflicts sea turtles worldwide is

Efforts to clean up the 2010 oil spill, from heavy equipment operation to nighttime lighting of beaches, disturbed loggerhead nesting sites.

Costa Rica's Jaguar Rescue Center helps animals such as leatherbacks return to healthy lives in the wild.

fibropapilloma, which produces tumors on the soft tissue of the turtles' head, flippers, and body. These growths can cover eyes and mouths, making seeing and eating difficult. Large tumors on flippers can impede swimming, and tumors that grow on internal organs can cause death. The disease was first identified in 1938, but it remained rare until recently. For decades, only a handful of turtles were found to have tumors, but since the early 2000s, hundreds of cases have been reported around the world. Researchers are struggling to learn why the instances of fibropapilloma are increasing, but they suspect that increased ocean pollution may play a major role.

Climate change affects sea turtles in many ways. A recent study by scientists at the University of Exeter's Marine Turtle Research Group in Great Britain found that, as Earth's surface temperatures have increased, the incidence of female loggerhead hatchlings has increased—in some cases, an entire clutch (or 100 to 150 eggs) will be female. If such a trend increases and more males are not produced, the species may eventually become unsustainable. In addition, if temperatures rise too much, sea turtle eggs will fail to hatch in the first place.

Because of changing weather patterns, sea turtles may get caught in currents that take them to colder climates, or they may become stranded on beaches that experience a sudden drop in temperature. When a sea turtle's body temperature falls and the animal is unable to warm up, it becomes what is called cold-stunned. Without treatment, the turtle will die. Wildlife hospitals and rehabilitation centers that specialize in sea turtle rescue can be found not only in coastal areas but also in cities with zoos that house sea turtles. With cooler weather occurring earlier in

Although veterinarians can often safely remove tumors from sea turtles, the growths persistently recur.

Supporters of the Georgia Sea Turtle Center can donate an engraved brick to the Turtle Walk.

Since 2007, the Georgia Sea Turtle Center on Jekyll Island has operated as the only hospital of its kind in the state.

the year in the southeastern United States in recent years, thousands of sea turtles have suffered or even died. The South Carolina Aquarium in Charleston, the Virginia Aquarium and Marine Center in Virginia Beach, and the Mote Marine Laboratory in Sarasota, Florida, are just a few of the places where cold-stunned sea turtles have been given a second chance at life.

Some facilities, such as the Georgia Sea Turtle Center, also specialize in rescuing and mending sea turtles that are injured or maimed in collisions with boats and propellers. Marine veterinarians have repaired broken shells, removed limbs too damaged to save, and performed therapy on sea turtles that have developed a syndrome commonly called "bubble butt." This happens when too much gas builds up inside a sea turtle's gut, causing the turtle's back end to float like a buoy and preventing the animal from reaching food on the seafloor. Weight therapy involves attaching diving weights to areas of a sea turtle's shell. Sometimes the turtles' internal balance can be restored and the turtle released back into the wild. If the therapy is unsuccessful, however, the sea turtles are placed in zoos or aquariums, where they must continue to be weighted.

Five of the seven sea turtle species are listed as endangered or critically endangered on the Red List of Threatened Species that is published annually by the International Union for Conservation of Nature (IUCN). Sea turtles face incredible pressure from not only human interference but also natural planetary changes. Only with the help of diligent protection of nesting sites and continued research and education on the needs of sea turtles can these unique animals ever hope to thrive in Earth's oceans once more.

Cracked shells caused by boat strikes can often be repaired with a special cement, as long as the cracks are not too deep.

ANIMAL TALE: THE TURTLE'S POOL

Many of the world's legendary stories are rooted in fact, including this one from Hawaii that tells about a special gift given to humans by a magical sea turtle on Punalu'u, a black sand beach on the Big Island of Hawaii.

Long ago, a volcano called Kilauea erupted, sending lava down the mountain toward the sea. When the lava reached the cold ocean water, it exploded into countless shards of black glass. For thousands of years, the ocean waves washed over the glass, and eventually a soft, black beach was formed.

The children often played on the beach, where the black sand was softer and warmer than any other sand on the island. When the sun went down and the children went home, the black beach was invisible in the darkness. One moonless night, a beautiful green sea turtle named Honu-po'o-kea emerged from the depths and dragged herself across the sand. She could see nothing in the dark, yet she knew the way to the very spot where she herself had hatched decades before. In this spot she dug a shallow hole in the sand, deposited a single, very special egg, and then carefully covered the nest. Honu-po'o-kea returned to the sea.

As the children continued to play on the beach, they were unaware that a special turtle egg was in the sand beneath their feet. Two months passed, and Honu-po'o-kea revisited Punalu'u. Her egg hatched, and a baby turtle the color of kauila wood—a beautiful tree found only in Hawaii— emerged from the black sand. As the children watched, Honu-po'o-kea dug another hole, this one very deep. Magically, fresh water sprang from the

hole, forming a pool. The baby turtle, whom Honu-po'o-kea named Kauila, crawled to the pool and dove in. All the children were thrilled and went to the pool to drink the clean, cold water.

Fresh water was difficult to collect on the island, so a freshwater pool on the beach was a wonderful convenience. All the islanders thanked Honu-po'o-kea for her gift of the pool and welcomed the little turtle Kauila to live in the pool as long as she wished. They named the beach Punalu'u, which means "diving pool."

Because Honu-po'o-kea was a magical turtle, the pool she created was magical, too. While in the pool, Honu-po'o-kea's daughter was a sea turtle, but when she left the pool during the day, she changed into a little girl who could play with the children. At night, when the children went home, Kauila returned to the pool and became a turtle again.

For many generations, the islanders continued to draw fresh drinking water from a number of pools on Punalu'u, and they were grateful to the magical sea turtle Honu-po'o-kea for her wonderful gift. Whenever the people saw bubbles rising from the pools—which happens in a natural well—they said that Kauila was sleeping deep below the surface.

One day, an earthquake struck the island, and massive waves crashed onto the beaches. The pools were washed away. Without the magical pools, Kauila could not transform into a human anymore. Though she could now visit the beaches only in her natural form as a sea turtle, the children still loved to come to the beaches to see her. To this day, green and hawksbill turtles regularly nest on Punalu'u beach.

GLOSSARY

archaeologists – people who study human history by examining ancient peoples and their artifacts

commercial – used for business and to gain a profit rather than for personal reasons

cultures – particular groups in a society that share behaviors and characteristics that are accepted as normal by that group

genetically – relating to genes, the basic physical units of heredity

Global Positioning System – a system of satellites, computers, and other electronic devices that work together to determine the location of objects or living things that carry a trackable device

herpetologists – people who study reptiles and their lives

hibernating – spending the winter in a sleeplike state in which breathing and heart rate slow down

incubate – to keep an egg warm and protected until it is time for it to hatch

invertebrates – animals that lack a backbone, including shellfish, insects, and worms

magnetic field – the invisible force that makes compass needles line up in a north-south direction

Mesoamerica – the area from central Mexico through Central America, including Belize, El Salvador, Guatemala, and Honduras

middens – mounds or pits used as trash dumps over many generations; they are of particular interest to archaeologists

migrations – regular, seasonal journeys from one place to another and then back again

monsoons – seasonal winds that bring rain in Southeast Asia and India

nutrients – substances that give an animal energy and help it grow

parasites – animals or plants that live on or inside another living thing (called a host) while giving nothing back to the host; some parasites cause disease or even death

plankton – microscopic algae and animals that drift or float in the ocean

poaching – hunting protected species of wild animals, even though doing so is against the law

zooplankton – tiny sea creatures (some microscopic) and the eggs and larvae of larger animals

SELECTED BIBLIOGRAPHY

ARKive. "Flatback turtle (*Natator depressus*)." http://www.arkive.org/flatback-turtle/natator-depressus/.

Davidson, Osha Gray. *Fire in the Turtle House: The Green Sea Turtle and the Fate of the Ocean*. New York: PublicAffairs, 2003.

Ruckdeschel, Carol, and C. Robert Shoop. *Sea Turtles of the Atlantic and Gulf Coasts of the United States*. Athens: University of Georgia Press, 2006.

Sea Turtle Conservancy. "Information About Sea Turtles, Their Habitats and Threats to Their Survival." http://www.conserveturtles.org/sea-turtle-information.php.

Spotila, James R. *Saving Sea Turtles: Extraordinary Stories from the Battle Against Extinction*. Baltimore: Johns Hopkins University Press, 2011.

——. *Sea Turtles: A Complete Guide to their Biology, Behavior, and Conservation*. Baltimore: Johns Hopkins University Press, 2004.

Stringer, Nick. *Turtle: The Incredible Journey*. DVD. West Sussex, UK: Big Wave Productions, 2009.

Note: Every effort has been made to ensure that any websites listed above were active at the time of publication. However, because of the nature of the Internet, it is impossible to guarantee that these sites will remain active indefinitely or that their contents will not be altered.

The more humans affect ocean life, the more sea turtles will need our help to survive.

INDEX